Measuring

Peter Patilla

Heinemann Library
Des Plaines, Illinois

© Reed Educational 2000 & Professional Publishing
Published by Heinemann Library,
an imprint of Reed Educational & Professional Publishing,
1350 East Touhy Avenue, Suite 240 West
Des Plaines, IL 60018

Customer Service 1-888-454-2279

Designed by AMR
Illustrations by Jessica Stockham (Beehive Illustration)
Originated by HBM Ltd., Singapore
Printed and bound by South China Printing Co., Hong Kong/China

04 03 02 01 00
10 9 8 7 6 5 4 3 2 1

Library of Congress Cataloging-in-Publication Data
Patilla, Peter.
    Measuring / Peter Patilla.
        p. cm. – (Math Links)
    Includes bibliographical references and index.
    Summary: Explores basic concepts of measurement, including linear measurement, weight, volume, as well as the units used to express them.
    ISBN 1-57572-965-2 (lib. bdg.)
    1. Mensuration Juvenile literature. [1. Measurement.]
    I. Title. II. Series: Patilla, Peter. Math links.
    QA465.P342 1999
    530.8—dc21   99-20367
                                          CIP

Acknowledgments

The Publishers would like to thank the following for permission to reproduce photographs:
Trevor Clifford, pgs. 4, 5, 7, 8, 9, 10, 11, 14, 15, 16, 17, 18, 19, 20, 21, 22, 23, 25, 27, 28, 29.

Cover photo: Trevor Clifford

Our thanks to David Kirkby for his comments in the preparation of this book.

Every effort has been made to contact copyright holders of any material reproduced in this book. Any omissions will be rectified in subsequent printings if notice is given to the Publisher.

Some words in this book are in bold, **like this.** You can find out what they mean by looking in the glossary. Look for the answers to questions in the green boxes on page 31.

Contents

Is It the Right Size? 4

Largest and Smallest 6

Opposites 8

Comparing Length 10

Measuring Length 12

Comparing Weight..........................14

Measuring Weight 16

Comparing Capacity 18

Measuring Capacity........................20

Comparing Volume 22

Comparing Temperature 24

Measuring Temperature 26

Comparing Size 28

Glossary...30

More Books to Read 30

Fact File 31

Answers 31

Index..32

Is It the Right Size?

too big   **too small**   **just right**

Sometimes things are too big. Sometimes they are too small. We like things to be just the right size.

4

Tops should fit onto bottoms so that things inside won't fall out.

Find the top that goes with each bottom.

Largest and Smallest

largest

smallest

same size

When things are next to each other, we can tell if they are about the same size. We can also see which is the largest and which is the smallest.

Here are many different objects. They are
different sizes.

Which is the largest object you can see? Which is
the smallest?

Opposites

tall ladder

little brush

short ladder

big brush

When we talk about sizes, we often use words that are opposites. We use words such as big and little or tall and short.

8

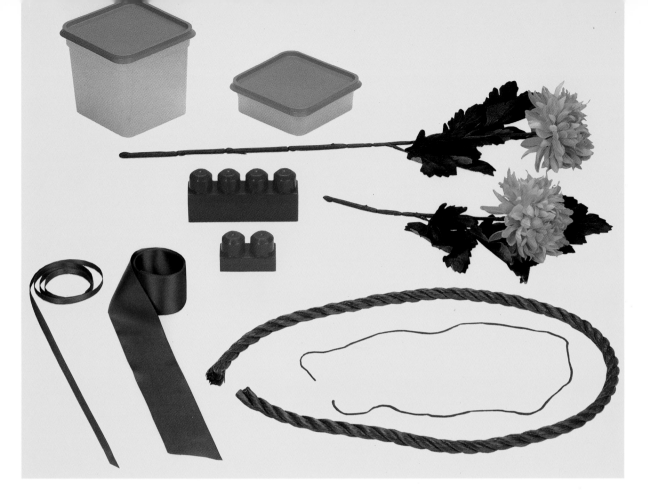

There are lots of opposites in this picture. We use words that tell about the pairs of objects—deep and shallow, wide and narrow, large and small, thick and thin, long and short.

Which pair of opposite words fits each pair of objects?

Comparing Length

Many years ago people used parts of their bodies to measure things. Sometimes they used their hands, but hands are different sizes. The measurements were not always the same.

10

These objects are measured with **standard units**.
Each standard unit is the same size.

What standard unit is being used? How
many units does each object measure?

11

Measuring Length

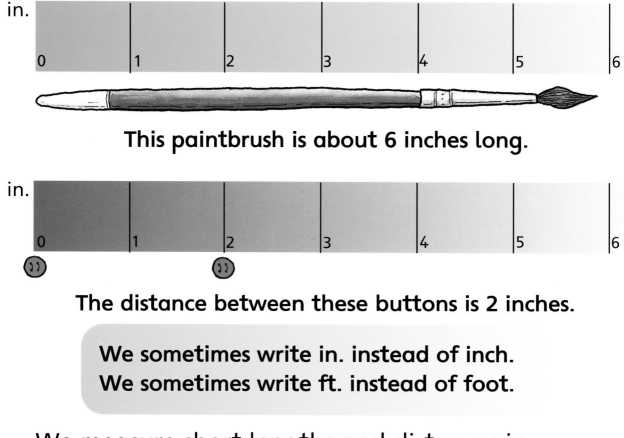

This paintbrush is about 6 inches long.

The distance between these buttons is 2 inches.

We sometimes write in. instead of inch.
We sometimes write ft. instead of foot.

We measure short lengths and distances in inches. We measure longer lengths in feet, yards, and miles.

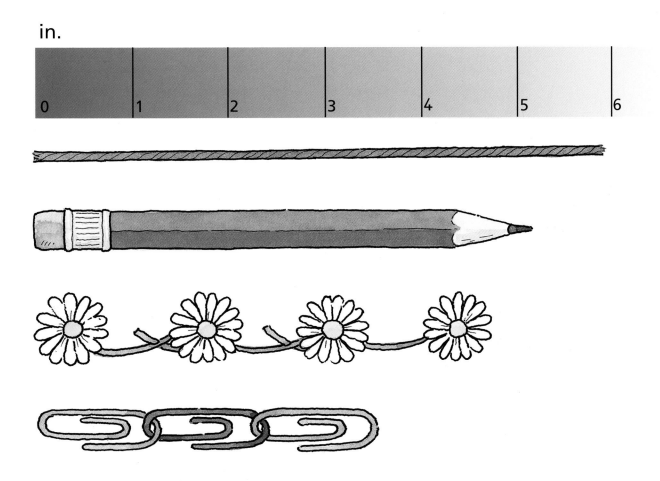

A reasonable guess is called an estimate. We sometimes use estimates when we don't need to have an exact measurement.

Estimate how many inches long each object is. Then use a ruler to measure each object.

Comparing Weight

same weight

heavier

lighter

Sometimes we pick things up to estimate if they are heavier, lighter, or about the same weight. We can use a **balance scale** to find out the exact weight. The heavier object will be on the lower side.

14

Bananas can be weighed on a balance scale.

Which bunches of bananas will be the heaviest?
Which bunch will be the lightest? Which bunches
will weigh about the same?

Measuring Weight

This is a balance scale and weights.

This is a scale with a dial.

We can use a **balance scale** and **weights** to find out how heavy something is. Each weight has a number written on it. We can also use a **scale** and read the weight on the dial.

Things that are light are weighed in ounces.
Things that are heavy are weighed in pounds.

Look at the objects. Which ones will be
weighed in ounces? In pounds?

Comparing Capacity

almost full

almost empty

half full

empty

full

Capacity is how much something will hold. Things can be full, empty, or somewhere in between. We can use liquid or dry things to find the capacity of containers.

Which container has greater capacity—the pitcher or the glass?

Measuring Capacity

All of these containers have the same amount of liquid in them. The shape of a container can make the same amount look different. But the shape does not change the amount.

Each of these containers has a different capacity.

We measure capacity in cups, pints, quarts, and gallons. Which containers will hold about a cup? Which container will hold a gallon?

Comparing Volume

Volume is the amount of space something takes up. Heavy things might only take up a little space. Light things might take up lots of space.

When we put things into a container, we have to think about how much space the things will take up.

Each pile of clothing has a different volume. Which pile will fit into the suitcase?

Comparing Temperature

Temperature is how hot, cold, or warm something is. Temperature is important for our bodies, for animals, for foods, and for plants.

When it is cold outside, we want to keep warm.

When it is hot, we want to keep cool.

Which clothes would keep us warm?

Which clothes would keep us cool?

Measuring Temperature

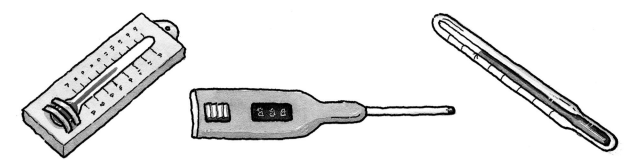

There are different thermometers for people and for things.

Temperature is measured in degrees.

Thermometers measure how hot or cold something is. A low number means something is cold. A high number means something is hot.

Cooking raises the temperature of food. Cooling or freezing lowers the temperature of food. Changing the temperature helps food last longer.

Which foods in this picture will have to be cooked before they can be eaten?

Comparing Size

Drawings and models can be larger, smaller, or the same size as the real thing.

Toy models may be smaller, larger, or the sa[me] size as the real thing.

Find the toys that are about the same siz[e as] the real thing. Find the toys that are sm[aller] than the real thing.

Glossary

balance scale simple machine used to compare the weight of two things

scale instrument for weighing things

standard unit measuring unit in which each unit is the same size. Same-size paper clips can be used as standard units.

temperature how hot or cold something is

thermometer instrument for measuring how hot something is in standard units called degrees

weight piece of metal that weighs a known amount used to measure the weight of other things

More Books to Read

...tt, Sally. *Measuring*. Austin, Tex.: Raintree Steck-...n, 1996.

...avid. *Measuring*. Crystal Lake, Ill.: Rigby ... Library, 1996.

...ctor. *How to Measure*. Austin, Tex.: Raintree ...n, 1995.

Fact File

Length: foot (ft.), inch (in.), yard (yd.), mile (mi.)

           1 foot = 12 inches

           1 yard = 3 feet

           1 mile = 5,280 feet

Weight: pound (lb.), ounce (oz.)

           1 pound = 16 ounces

Capacity: gallon (gal.) quart (qt.), pint (pt.), cup (c.)

           1 gallon = 4 quarts

           1 quart = 2 pints

           1 pint = 2 cups

Temperature: degrees (°), Fahrenheit (F), Celsius (C)

     freezing water = 32° F = 0° C

      boiling water = 212° F= 100° C

Answers

page 7	largest: green car, smallest: black & white car
page 9	deep and shallow boxes, long and short flowers, large and small bricks, wide and narrow ribbon, thick and thin necklaces
page 11	paperclip—potted plant is 11 paper clips tall, glass is 8 paper clips around, pencil is 6 paper clips long
page 13	string is about 6 in. long, daisies are about 4 3/4 in. long, paperclips are about 3 1/2 in. long.
page 15	heaviest: 5-banana bunch, lightest: 2-banana bunch, same weight: 4-banana bunches
page 17	bricks and oranges–weighed in pounds, cotton balls and feathers–weighed in ounces
page 19	the pitcher
page 21	hold a cup—pitcher, ladle, cup, bowl holds a gallon—bucket
page 23	pile 3
page 25	warm: boots, coat, ski hat, sweater, gloves, scarf cool: straw hat, tank top, swim trunks, shorts, sandals
page 27	snow peas, chicken, hot dogs, fish

31

Index

balance scale 14–15, 16, 30

cup 21, 31

degree 26, 31

foot 12, 31

gallon 20, 31

inch 12–13, 31

opposites 8, 9

ounce 16–17, 31

pint 21, 31

pound 16–17, 31

quart 20, 31

scales 14–16, 30

standard unit 11, 30

temperature 24–27, 30

thermometer 26, 30

yard 12, 31